*The
Family
of the*
Priest

The Family of the Priest

La Famiglia del Prete

DOMENIC MEFFE

Copyright © 2014 by Domenic Meffe. All rights reserved.

ISBN 978-0-9937345-0-2

www.domenicmeffe.com

email: info@domenicmeffe.com

Text by Bernadette Hardaker, LifeStories, www.lifestories.ca

Book design and typesetting by Daniel Crack, Kinetics Design, www.kdbooks.ca

Illustrations by Melodie Papp, www.melodiepapp.com

Names and dates are based on the best information available and gathered at the time family members were interviewed over a period of many years.

*For my family and friends –
that they understand
where we come from.*

Contents

Origins 1

The Meffe Lineage 13

What's in a Name? 15

Madonna 21

A Special Gift 35

Tragedy 57

A New Life 65

From Joy to Rage 79

And Now 91

Acknowledgements 99

Torella del Sannio

CHAPTER ONE

Origins

I heard the wind rustle through the olive groves. My mouth tasted the dust of the roadside. In the distance we could see the three towers guarding the medieval castle that gives our town of two hills its name.

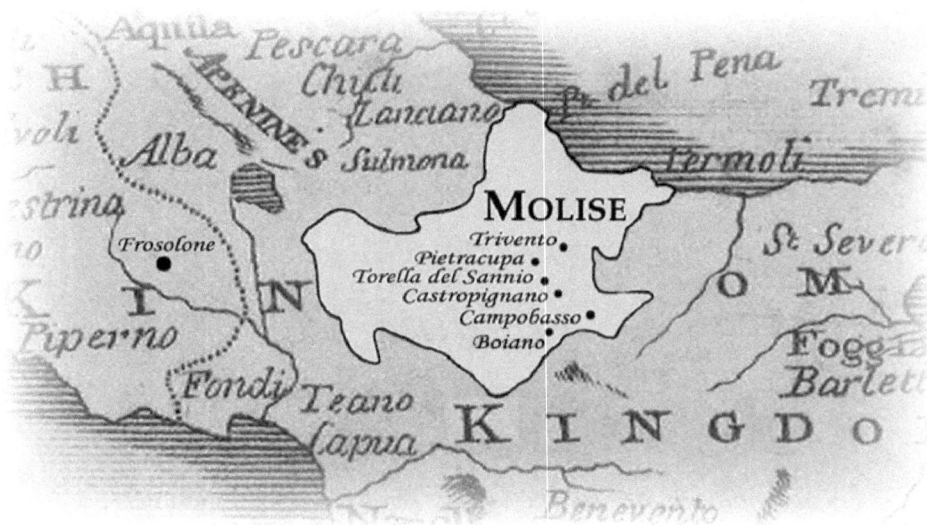

Region of Molise, Italy

My nonno never told me whether our ancestor, the priest, really killed his wife so long ago. Every day, he and I walked with our dogs on la costa, the public grazing land close to our home. We tended the 60 sheep and goats belonging to my father and zio Giuseppe and every day, he told me bits and pieces of our family story. We walked from sunrise to sunset, hand in hand, the ancient Domenicantonio and the young Domenico, stopping for a crust of bread, a bite of cheese, and a sip of wine at noon, and returning home as my mother's cries called us in for the evening meal.

At seven, my walks with nonno were replaced by school and the struggle of sitting still for hours at a desk, waiting to be set free to jostle and kick a ball with the other boys.

~ The Family of the Priest ~

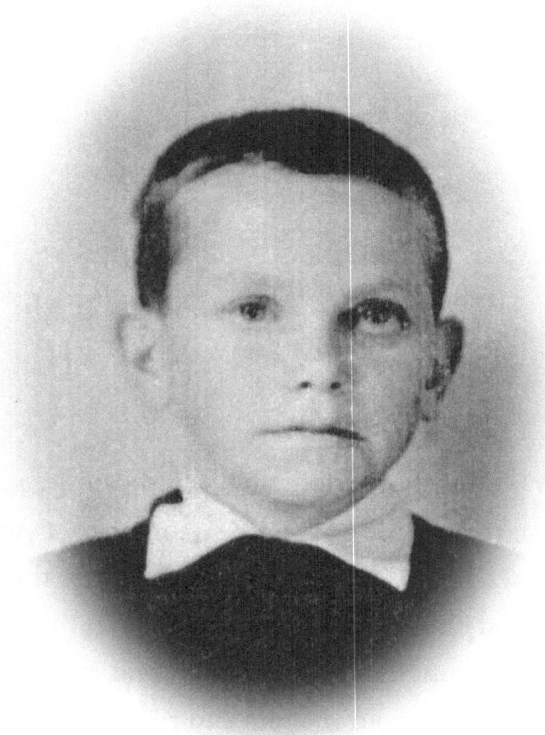

*The little boy who listened to
his grandfather's tales — Domenic at eight.*

At nine, my father left for Canada, looking for prosperity like so many other men from the village: a new start in a new world. Italy's economy was shattered after WWII. In our isolated region, there were no jobs and, it seemed, no future. My father wanted so much more for us than what our tiny farm could produce –

The Family of the Priest

only 10 hectares remained of the great estate once held by my ancestors – divided among so many sons over the generations that we were just getting by. We had no electricity or running water and little food. Sometimes supper was a salad of onions and chicory.

At nine, no longer a child, I took my place beside my mother and my older brother Francesco and worked the farm. When my mother went to sell cheese or chickens or a calf, I went along with her, quickly learning the fine art of deal making. When school was over at one each afternoon, I ran to the fields to weed or hoe or pick – whatever needed to be done. Then at night, I fed the animals, cleaned out the manure, and laid fresh straw at their feet. I was always in trouble at school, because there was never time for homework. Wandering the hills with the sheep, I used to wonder about this place, Canada, so far away it might as well have been the moon, and I worried, *Would I ever see my father again?*

The summer after papà left, nonno became ill. He cried often, lamenting, "I'll never see my son again!" He stopped his long walks on the land. When he came to the table, he stirred his soup and ignored my uncle's fine wine. We all tried to reach him: I was excited about the new lambs about to be born; my older brother asked him which seeds to buy, when we should plant, which trees needed cutting – subjects which nonno would freely regale us with in the past. Mamma passed on the concerns of local folk she met in the fields, who worried about how he was doing. Whenever a letter came from papà, she read him the funny bits. Like when he wrote there were more cars in Toronto than potatoes in Molise! (There were only a couple of cars in Torella at the time.) His teeth or lack thereof – he'd worn dentures for years – were also a popular subject. My sister used to cook him steaks for dinner in Toronto. He'd say, "When I was young my teeth were good and I had no meat. Now I have meat and no teeth to chew it!" Canadian bread was a problem too – so gooey it stuck to his dentures. If he tried to dip it in wine, it stayed in the glass!

But none of our efforts made a difference. The being who sat head bent and silent, grew more and more frail, and it wasn't long before nonno stopped leaving his bed altogether. We tried to keep him comfortable, but he was tired and disinterested as though done with life.

By late the following winter, only 14 months after my father's departure, my nonno was dead and, at almost 11, I learned that there are not enough tears to mourn someone so special. I dreamt of him every day, and I still do. My grandfather could barely read or write, but he possessed great wisdom and sometimes at meetings with bankers and lawyers, I find his words coming from my mouth.

In 1965, the rest of us joined my father, Giustino, in Toronto and my grandfather's stories slept in the back of my head as our family worked in this new life to make our own Canadian dream.

Six of us shared a basement apartment. I tried school for a time, but it was too hard. When I did learn enough English to understand the taunts of my classmates, I fought back. The nuns strapped me regularly, but my hands were so calloused from work that I never cried. I always had at least two jobs, shovelling driveways or selling photo portraits at weddings after a full day's work in the factory. I wanted to make money, but I wanted to go downtown and have fun too. I'd come home at three in the morning and be up again at six. My shoes were on my feet 18 hours a day and, once, my feet became so bruised and swollen I couldn't walk.

It was so easy to get caught up in our second life in Canada and forget all that we had left behind. At 19, I married a girl from Torella. At 20, I bought my first restaurant. At 34, I built my first hotel. There was so little time in those early days. Yet in those quiet moments after the relatives left on a Sunday night, that great longing for our birthplace was sometimes so strong it hurt. We could not deny our heritage and, eventually, Molise pulled us back like metal filings to a magnet.

And so, in 1982 we flew to Rome. My wife, Carmela, and I along with our two children (our third not yet born) were greeted and endlessly hugged by my cousin, Domenicantonio, and his wife. The words tumbled out so fast that we could barely breathe as we tried to cram the news of nearly two decades into those first few moments on Italian soil. The children stood back shyly until they were caught up in the pinches and embraces of relatives they'd never met. Somehow, we all fit into my cousin's car – I had forgotten how small cars were here! Then, as the fatigue of the journey started to press against my forehead, the children drifted off to sleep to the murmur of the women going through the long list of births, deaths, and marriages.

We took the long way back on narrow mountain roads. Fixing my gaze on the rugged Molise countryside, I heard the wind rustle through the olive groves and watched as it rippled across the fields of gold-tipped wheat. My mouth tasted the dust rising from the roadside, as I basked in the heat of the midday sun. Once again, I inhaled the air of my homeland – my blood oxygenated with the breath of the land that had

— *The Family of the Priest* —

given life to me and my ancestors all these centuries. I shivered with pleasure and anticipation.

Suddenly, my cousin pulled to a stop at the side of the road and announced with a wave of his hand, "There's Torella!" We were near Frosolone, a nearby mountain-top village, and 15 kilometres in the distance through the slight haze, we could see the three towers guarding the medieval castle that gives our town its name, and beside the castle, San Nicola's church with its great bell tower. That bell was the centre of our lives. Not only did it call us to pray, it warned us of danger, announced celebrations and tragedies, and counted the hours as sure as the sun rises and sets. Then winding around the hills, the crowd of thick-walled houses clustered – their grey-tiled roofs breaking up the uniformity of the hand-chiseled stone, bleached by the centuries. And finally, where stone met soil, the fields patched green and yellow, just as I remembered. My heart choked in my throat and my eyes filled. There it was, Torella del Sannio. So quiet. So beautiful. My home.

When I was a boy in the 1950s, before everyone began to leave in search of new opportunities in Argentina, Canada and the United States, there were nearly 3,000 Torellesi. Today, 800 remain, all of them descendants of the 360 families of the area. This was not the case in the late 1700s when village life centred on the fortunes of far fewer families. And it was this life that I wanted to explore with my Italian relatives, to remember my grandfather's stories and put to rest lingering doubts around our family name.

The moment I stepped out of the car in Torella and touched the ground, a primal energy vibrated through me, and the once familiar seemed wondrous. *What secrets lay hidden within these eternal walls and along these narrow streets? What stories could they tell?* I felt intensely happy, but at the same time, full of regret. I never believed I would come back and here I was! Yet I had forgotten my grandfather's stories, abandoned my past, and had done nothing to protect and preserve our history for the next generation and the generations to come. My children knew so little of their heritage.

That night we slept in nonno's 200-year-old house. At six the next morning, I left my sleeping family to meet my uncle and to walk the same path I walked with my grandfather, back to the past. Zio told me the stories as he remembered them and slowly, I began to remember – memories echoing deeply in a forgotten place in my heart.

My parents had told me things when I was a child, but what child really listens to a parent's stories? When

The Family of the Priest

a grandfather calmly takes you by the hand and speaks, you absorb his words completely and their message goes straight to the heart.

Our story centres on an earlier Domenicantonio Meffe, my direct ancestor, in fact, my great-great-great-grandfather. He was clever and much loved; an only child who grew into an ambitious young man. Mere months before a bishop's thumb crossed his forehead, lips, and heart with holy oil and before he spoke the final vows to become a Roman Catholic priest, he renounced his vocation. Instead, he married, fathered children, and took over the family estate. By all accounts, he was a great success. Yet despite his accomplishments, he died a confused, heartbroken old man, convinced he had stabbed his beloved wife, Teresa, to death.

An autopsy was never done, no murder conviction, not even a charge laid against him. Honour killings were an unspoken fact of life to protect the social order. Honour, as a defence, was only struck from the Italian law books just over 30 years ago.

Murder is nothing to be proud of, which is probably why no one else has recorded our story, yet understanding the circumstances of my ancestor's actions were important to me. In the end, how much of our story is fact and how much is speculation is difficult to say. My aim is to present the straightest path to the truth and let others decide.

"My grandfather's stories seemed as old as his boots."

The Meffe Lineage

Domenicantonio
Grandfather of the Priest

≀

Giustino 1760 ~ 1816
Father of the Priest

≀

Domenicantonio 1784 ~ circa 1860
The Priest

≀

Donato 1823 ~ circa 1883
Second son of the Priest

≀

Giustino 1846 ~ 1914
Grandson of the Priest

≀

Domenicantonio 1885 ~ 1962
Great~Grandson of the Priest

≀

Giustino 1914 ~ 1992
Great~Great Grandson of the Priest

≀

Domenico 1951 ~
Great~Great~Great Grandson of the Priest

CHAPTER TWO

What's in a Name?

I am the fourth Domenico in living memory in my branch of the family and I may be the last to remember the details of the story that brands us.

IN the old days, it was common in Italy to distinguish different branches of large families by giving them nicknames, usually for something good, but sometimes for something stupid!

In Grassano, in the province of Matera to the south of us, there is a story of a letter-carrier in 1937 who was said to have fathered 50 children. His nickname was the "king", most likely in recognition of his virility, and naturally, his sons were known as the "princes."

In our village, the nicknames could be unforgiving, commemorating an ancestor's physical ailment or a mistake that would rather be forgotten. Our family has been fortunate. A professor is a very highly regarded profession, so my cousin Domenicantonio's branch of

The Family of the Priest

the family is known as 'la famiglia del professore'. For five generations, I have belonged to 'la famiglia del prete', the family of the priest. In a Catholic country, having a priest in the family was the highest honour imaginable, the source of endless pride and unequalled respect. Not only would it confer honour on that particular family but the entire home town the priest came from, so it was something to be guarded and cherished by the entire tribe.

I am the fourth Domenico in living memory in my branch of the family and I may be the last to remember the details of the story that brands us, the story that was passed to my grandfather from his father and then to me. Today, only the old people refer to us as 'la famiglia del prete'. Those under 70 don't remember.

The surname Meffe dates back five centuries. Prior to 1780, our branch was nicknamed for an earlier Meffe ancestor named Feliciani, a successful man with most likely a happy disposition, as the root of the name comes from the Latin word *felix* for happy. The grandfather of my ancestor, the priest, was Domenicantonio Meffe 'della famiglia del Feliciani'. He was a major landowner holding hundreds of tomoli in a huge area around our village. (Tomoli is the word we use in our local dialect to measure the land.) He employed dozens of contadini to work his fields, tend his animals, and care for his vineyards, for after land, barrels of wine were a measurement of wealth. This was the privileged world into which my ancestor, the priest, was born.

My principal sources of information were the older members of my family, my father who died in 1992, and his siblings – my uncles Giuseppe, Clemente and Angelo who died in 2012, and my aunts Assunta and Ursula. Of that generation, Giuseppe is the eldest surviving member of the family and at 98 is still living in his home. I spoke with zia Assunta not long before

Domenic's grandparents, Domenicantonio and Petronilla Meffe, circa 1930.

her death in 1997. She remembered the most, because after she married and left home as a young girl of 20, she learned what others were saying about our family – the whispers speculating why he had left the priesthood, the theories of what took his wife's life when she appeared so healthy, and the question of why an overseer on the estate left so suddenly after her death. Even late in life, when the priest was a lonely, old man passing his days on a battered bench in the sunshine of the piazza, insisting to anyone who would listen that he was responsible for his wife's death, most made little of his ravings, a man so close to the grave.

What remains true is one of zia Assunta's strongest childhood memories. The family is sitting around the heavy kitchen table by flickering candlelight. Despite the heat of the fire that warms their work-weary muscles and leadens their eyes, the young ones still have the energy to beg their grandfather, "Tata, tell us a story!" And that is where we begin.

CHAPTER THREE
Madonna

*As he approached a large olive tree, he noticed
a young woman fast asleep in its shade. He had never
seen her before and, it's said, he was so impressed
by her beauty, it took his breath away.*

As the eldest son of a rural Italian family in the late 18th century, the fate of young Giustino Meffe del Feliciani was determined at his first breath – he would work like a dog until it was his turn to manage the family estate. He was as much a prisoner of the land as the contadini his father employed and the same fatalistic acceptance characterized them all, like a shrug of the shoulder, as if to say, "What else could my life be?"

Like most young boys, Giustino hated girls when he was small and couldn't stop thinking of them when he was just a few years older. Talk of marriage wouldn't occur until he had proven himself as an able successor to the estate and until his parents had arranged for him to marry a girl of equal social standing with a respectable dowry.

~ *The Family of the Priest* ~

Giustino's day began at dawn when he was summoned by his father to the breakfast table. Authority to his father was absolute, his word unquestioned. Every day, as he dipped the grilled cornbread his mother silently served into his cup of warm milk, his father proclaimed the list of chores Giustino was expected to complete. Year in and year out, the chores were the same, only the order changed with the seasons. And every day, his father repeated the litany of the land. "The estate must come first. After all, it's our life." Giustino did not linger at the table.

One glorious morning, Giustino headed to the small barn in a nearby pasture to feed the animals and clean their stalls as usual. By noon, he had finished his inside work. Fastening his pitchfork to the saddle, he mounted his horse to make his way to a tract of land his father owned not far from the next village of Castropignano.

The sun beat him with the sharp, sweet smell of fresh hay as he picked his way across the fields to the farm. The heat made him drowsy. Halfway between the two villages, as he approached the track shepherds used to guide their flocks up to the mountains in the summer heat and down to the sea in the winter cold, he stopped. *Are those sheep I hear on il tratturo?* This made no sense to the young man. It was too late to move a flock. Then, as if summoned, he was surrounded by a dozen or so of the bleating animals. *They must have wandered off from that crazy old man's place. Best to keep moving*, he thought, *or risk being accused of thievery.*

As he approached a large olive tree, he noticed a young woman fast asleep in its shade, a half-opened book and the remnants of a meal by her side. He had never seen her before and, it's said, he was so impressed by her beauty, it took his breath away. She was maybe 18, slim, dark-haired and "as beautiful as a Madonna." He didn't want to disturb her, but he was curious to know who she was.

He dismounted and carefully led his horse to the tree. Just a few steps from her, he stopped abruptly. There was no breeze to riffle the grass. Then, he saw the snake! A viper as long as his arm, brown and fat, was slowly slithering towards the girl. Her lovely face rested on the ground framed by her extended arm, her mouth, slightly open in deep slumber. He knew the tales – snakes crawling into people's mouths and clothing to avoid the heat. When I was a boy looking after the sheep in 1959, my mother warned me not to fall asleep outside; snakes had the power to hypnotize their victims!

Whether or not Giustino believed the old wives' tales, he could not risk it. Deliberately, he reached for the saddle and untied the pitchfork, his eyes never leaving his prey. The horse nickered and stamped nervously. "Shhhh!" Giustino slowly stepped into the snake's path, positioned the fork, and drove it into the snake's head, burying it in the ground.

The action woke the girl with a start – a stranger with a pitchfork poised above her! Naturally, she screamed. In the same moment, Giustino blurted out confused apologies. The snake pinned to the ground was quick evidence. It was then her turn to apologize and effusively thank the boy who had saved her life. She offered him a drink from her flask. He thanked her formally and drank deeply. She kept her eyes nervously on a spot below his left knee. There was nothing more to say. A proper young man and a virtuous young woman didn't just strike up a conversation in those days. They said their goodbyes and parted. There were chores to finish.

That night at the supper table, Giustino told his parents about the sheep, the snake, and the beautiful girl. The experience had obviously made a strong impression and his parents were curious to know the girl's identity, but he had been too shy to ask. His father gruffly snorted, "Don't worry about some girl. What was she doing out there on her own anyway? Is she some kind of tramp?" His mother knew otherwise – her son was smitten. She would ask her sister-in-law when they met at mass the next morning.

Years later, Giustino would say that day changed his life forever. For the first time, he felt like a man. Did his Madonna, he wondered, think of him as a fine, young, *Christian* man?

For three months, Giustino could think of nothing but the beautiful girl. He drove his parents wild with his incessant talk of seeing her again. As the son of the Don, and coming from such a prominent family, it was not seemly for him to go to Castropignano himself and inquire directly about her identity. He could only hope that fate would bring them together.

In late summer, on another hot day with no hint of wind, Giustino rode heavily between the fields. Both horse and man were soaked with sweat. He touched his knee to the horse's side and the animal headed for relief in the direction of one of the local ponds. There were so many sheep in Torella del Sannio that sometimes neighbours had to schedule when to take their animals to the water. The practise was to throw the sheep into the pond and as they swam, the water cleansed their fleece. Sometimes they did this three or four times before the sheep were ready to be shorn. This particular day the ponds should have been quiet.

As Giustino came closer, he heard muffled voices. He walked his horse towards the large boulders that surrounded the waterway and tethered it to a young willow tree. The horse snorted. "Quiet," he whispered. "Your turn will come."

As he advanced through the underbrush, he spied two women giggling and shushing each other as they splashed in the cool water. *What a vision!* Giustino thought, as he settled into his hiding spot to enjoy the young women enjoying their bath. Some say he watched for a time and then jumped in to startle them. Others say he silently hid their clothes and relished their naked distress. I think he stayed where he was. No matter. The ending of the story is the always the same.

When the women came out of the water, he saw clearly that one of them was the girl he'd rescued, the girl who had lodged herself so firmly in his head these last few months. His heart was pounding, his throat parched, his breath evaporated. He couldn't believe he was seeing her again. And what a way to see her! Like a miracle, so beautiful, so full of life, so deliciously unencumbered by clothing!

Not wanting to embarrass her, Giustino retreated. *I have to work harder to find this girl and meet her properly or I will never rest.* He began making excuses to leave his chores early and go to the market in Castropignano. Suddenly, he was interested in attending mass at the nearby village church and found new enthusiasm to participate reverently in the many feast days that marked the summer religious calendar. Anticipation gnawed at patience as the days and weeks went by, plotting new opportunities for a chance meeting. This may sound awkward and contrived, and it was, but that is how young people courted in those days.

Over many months, Giustino learned that her name was Maria and that she was the daughter of another landowner. They probably bumped into each other once or twice on a fine evening as she strolled around the piazza on the arm of one of her widowed aunts. They'd shyly exchange a few pleasantries, always under the protective eye of the black-veiled vedove.

Giustino's mother had also made her enquiries and decided that the girl Maria would be an acceptable wife for her prized boy, and so, she began to work on her husband. Whenever the boy sighed and looked dreamily into the distance, Giustino's father shouted, "Get your head out of the clouds! There's work to be done!"

As she watched her son's strong, young back move across the yard, she turned to her husband, "Why not face the fact, Dom, he needs a wife. He's like a young bull panting for a cow."

"We don't need the distraction right now. There is too much to be done. We'll be seeding soon."

"But Dom, remember when we were that age? Nothing could keep you off me. He is blood of your blood. The girl is strong. She will give us many grandsons. And she is devout. It's said God speaks to her."

"I don't know. Give me more of that wine."

"I'll give you something better." The older man laughed and followed his wife into their room.

Eventually, Giustino summoned the courage to ask his father's permission to talk of marriage with Maria's father. At his future father-in-law's they talked of weather and crops and whose land was more fertile. Then, as he was about to leave, Giustino formally asked for permission to visit Maria. Of course, the young people were never left alone. Maria's mother or married older sister or cousin – someone – was always working in the background, well within earshot.

After a respectable amount of time and a requisite number of silent visits, Giustino requested her hand. And after the fathers had wrestled over the terms of the dowry, then raised a glass to seal the bargain, it was official. Maria's mother was rapturous. The son of the famiglia del Feliciani! What a blessing. This union would bring much good fortune and honour to Maria's family. It was the match all good mothers of the region dreamed of for their daughters.

Wedding preparations began immediately. For weeks, fingers flew – embroidering the fine blouse and mantle for the bride and preparing the food for the marriage feast. The groom sent the bride gold earrings and a necklace to wear on her wedding day. The bride sent back a fine ram, a new olive press, and the deed for 30 tomoli that had been part of her mother's dowry. The night before the wedding, the young men of the village serenaded the bride outside her window. Then, climbing the ladder, the groom sang of love and desire. He presented her with a bouquet of red poppies and helped her through the window to the first of many feasts.

In about 1782, not very long after their introduction by a snake, Maria and Giustino were married.

── *The Family of the Priest* ──

On the wedding day, the groom and his family walked the six kilometres from Torella del Sannio to meet the bride and her family in Castropignano. The wedding party processed through the narrow streets followed by family, friends, and the rest of the village. They packed into the church for blessings, prayers, and incense, and then all poured out of the church to the piazza where tables were laden with the best foods of the region – delicate pasta with savoury stuffing, cavatelli and tacozze, herb-roasted lamb, bowls of olives, figs, and sweetened almonds, caciocavallo, and scamorza, freshly baked loaves of bread with pitchers of olive oil for dipping, and the famous dried meats of the region, capicollo, soppressa and ventricina. Of course, there was wine and dancing until dawn.

In the middle of the merriment, the bridal couple slipped away to the groom's home where crisp white sheets on a freshly stuffed mattress waited to receive them. The next morning they would be reviewed by Giustino's mother, verifying the virginity of his bride.

The young couple settled immediately into the ageless rhythm of the land. Giustino went back to his chores and Maria moved from her mother's house to her mother-in-law's. The two women got along well. Maria fed the chickens and pigs, scrubbed the floors

The Family of the Priest

twice a day, did the washing, and prepared the meals for the family. She brewed chamomile for her mother-in-law to ease the older woman's pains, and rubbed her head when tea was not enough. And she went to mass every day. Even Giustino's father grew to love the young woman he once called a whore.

People had always said that Maria was so kind she could have been a nun. Giustino was proud of his beautiful, pious, new wife. How could her goodness be anything but a blessing?

There was but one blemish on the fruit. Maria did not immediately conceive and when she did, the child withered in her womb. A second pregnancy and a third followed, but the bleeding came well before a child could survive.

Maria prayed constantly to the Virgin as she worked. She lit candles to the Virgin's mother, Santa Elisabetta, the patron saint of pregnant women. She confessed every ill thought and perceived misdeed, and no matter how she felt, daily she climbed the many steps to the church of San Nicola to eat the bread of life.

Finally, late in about 1784, her prayers were answered. After a long and difficult birth, their first child, a son, was born. He was named Domenicantonio, after Giustino's father. The two men celebrated their good fortune late into the night, while the exhausted mother cradled her tiny boy.

"Thank you Madre," she whispered. She felt great warmth overcome her and, certain this was a response from the Virgin, she made a secret vow. If the Virgin would let her boy thrive, she would dedicate him to God.

It was a risky promise for a mother to make, especially as the years passed and it became apparent that no more children were forthcoming. This caused the couple great sadness, but the boy's lively spirit lifted theirs and they poured all their hopes and energy into the young Domenicantonio.

Maria took the boy to church, not just every Sunday but every weekday. Giustino, who had by this time taken over the estate, wasn't convinced this was such a good idea. He used to joke, "What are you trying to do? Turn my son into a priest?" In a few years, the joke would not be so funny.

CHAPTER FOUR

A Special Gift

*W*hen it seemed it might be too late in the day for them to leave, Fra Marco announced, "We must go!" The boy looked at his mother, and shrugged slightly. "Well, I guess it's time," Maria said, smiling tightly.

As time passed, the two forces that guided the boy's life grew stronger, and the potential for conflict intensified. Giustino became more and more anxious to teach his son the ways of the land, while Maria pushed harder for the boy to excel in literature, theology, and mathematics. She didn't want to see her son nailed to the soil like her husband and he couldn't understand why the boy was reluctant to accept his patrimony. Each professed to have the boy's best interest at heart. Domenicantonio, a devoted son, spent his childhood trying to balance their competing desires and please them both.

Maria appeared to have the advantage. When the boy was not at mass, he was at school and when he was not at school, he was reading any book he could find, starting with the Bible. This delighted his mother and, as the boy excelled, she grew increasingly confident that this would be his vocation.

Giustino was often frustrated. Finding so little opportunity to be with his son, he was constantly yelling at the boy for not properly doing this job or that when they were together. He railed, too, at his wife. Why was she turning the boy against him? Could book learning put food on the table? Giustino saw only one purpose for his son's life – to take over the farm and enhance the wealth of the family. He was barely aware of himself repeating the very words his father had daily drummed into his head. As he approached middle age, Giustino now understood his father's fixation on the farm.

"Would God come down and provide for us?" Giustino used to say. "Not in my lifetime." And any talk to the contrary was pure nonsense. His son's religious attentions simply meant one less pair of hands to manage the land and less supervision of the many farm hands needed to run the estate.

As the years went by, the farm work eroded Giustino's energy; once happy conversations between husband and wife were replaced with sniping, wearing them down until they sat, more often than not, in hostile silence.

The boy wondered what more he could do to make his parents happy.

Normally, by age 12, a child's lot in life would be set, and for a time, this imminent birthday gave Giustino hope. He was ready to take back his son, but when the day came, Maria dug in her heels and insisted Domenicantonio continue his studies. The parents renewed their bickering with the boy caught in the middle. *I have a responsibility to help my father, but how can I disappoint my precious mamma?*

At the end of a particularly long day, as Giustino settled down to eat his bowl of scattone, Maria quietly informed her husband, "I have been speaking to the parish priest about our boy. He thinks…"

Giustino slammed his wooden spoon on the table and thundered, "Is this what all this has been about? All this book learning and church going? You and that black-robed swine have been conspiring against me all these years? You want to steal my son, my only hope for a place I have sweated over since I was a boy…you…you…."

Anger stalled his tongue as he sat glaring at his wife. Maria stared back, arms crossed, sure in her righteousness. Domenicantonio stormed out of the room. What was he to do?

Maria said nothing. As the days slipped by, the preoccupied father kept about his business, hoping that this priest idea would never again be raised.

Around his mother the boy remained quiet and obedient, almost passive. With his father he became increasingly brash and aggressive, prone to swearing. This behaviour reassured Giustino. As far as he was concerned, it was further proof that his son was ill-suited to the priesthood.

But Maria was a woman of great patience. She knew she had God, all his heavenly angels, and saints on her side. Here on earth, the local parish priest was her great ally. He had watched the boy's growing devotion and dedication as an altar server. He knew the boy was thoroughly versed in the Holy Scriptures, and it was only a matter of time before Domenicantonio came to the attention of the rural priest's superiors, which is how Giustino found himself in his kitchen one day pouring his best wine to, not one, but two priests.

The senior priest, who had ridden the 20 kilometres from Trivento by mule, made a strong case. "Signore, at 14, your boy shows an exceptional giftedness, far superior to most boys his age. It should be encouraged and so we would like to offer him a place at the monastery school."

"Are you saying you want my son to be a priest?"

"If it is God's will, yes."

Giustino shook his head, fighting to keep his temper leashed.

"You look troubled, Signor Meffe."

He locked eyes with the old priest. "How far is this school?" he growled. "My son is only a boy. How is he going to get there? Are you going to take him?"

"It's not so far. Your son would be under the care of the monks at Trivento."

"In other words, he'll be gone for months at a time! How the hell am I supposed to run a farm without my son?" Giustino turned and fixed his glare on Maria. "This is your doing. I hope you're satisfied, putting these big ideas into his head."

"Now Giustino," the parish priest interjected, "don't you think you are being too harsh?"

"It is not your place to judge me," Giustino roared. "I work from sunrise to sunset. What the hell do you do? Read books. Sprinkle holy water. Pray!" He spat out the last word like a curse. Afraid he would completely lose control, he bolted from the room, slamming the farmhouse door behind him.

The Family of the Priest

Giustino waved his arms in frustration as he strode across the farmyard. *How have we come to this? I am shouting at my beautiful Maria, so sweet and so good. She doesn't deserve this. I should have encouraged the boy more. I should have found other ways to have him with me. I should have been firmer. It is not Maria's fault. She is doing what she thinks is God's work. How can I argue with a saint? How can I give up on my son? How can I keep this damn farm going?*

Halfway to the barn, he stopped, turned, and walked back to the house to crouch out of sight under the kitchen window.

"Please forgive my husband," he heard Maria beg. "He works so hard and he worries about the farm and the contadini. Lately, he has been preoccupied with teaching our son how to tend the vines. It's really quite an art, knowing how to prune the vines and learning how to get the most from the land. My husband sees himself as a teacher too, but he has other things to teach our son. Maybe he feels that you're invading his domain. More wine?"

Just then, Giustino opened the door and re-entered the kitchen. "Yes, yes, give our guests more wine. We may not have enough hands on the damn farm to pour it the next time they visit."

Then Giustino sighed, "Look," his shoulders dropping, "You decide what the hell you want. I've got work to do. Just let me know where he'll be and how often he can come home – so I don't forget what he looks like."

Giustino opened the door and walked quietly toward the fields of waving wheat. *You can't argue with your wife when she has Rome on her side.*

In the following days, Maria, recognizing the huge concession Giustino had made, prayed steadily for advice. She knew she had to do everything she could to reconcile her husband and son in the time they had left together. Every morning, she encouraged Domenicantonio to spend the day with his father. He went reluctantly at first, but grew more willing. Hard work slowly built respect between the father and son, and for the first time in years, the air seemed lighter around the supper table. Giustino was grateful for Maria's efforts and flickers of familiar affection resurfaced.

The summer flew by. Soon, Domenicantonio would be leaving for the monastery. Giustino surveyed the harvest – well underway – it promised to be a good year. "Perhaps it's not so bad that my fine, young son serves God."

The following week, on a bright fall morning, mother and son watched a cart rattle towards the farmhouse. A friar in a greasy brown cassock layered in dust heaved his considerable weight to the ground to greet his audience.

"Buongiorno! I am Fra Marco, here to pick up the boy."

"Welcome Brother. Come in and rest. You must be exhausted. Domenicantonio, water the brother's mule and give it a bit of grain."

Turning to the friar, "Would you care to wash the road from your brow?" she invited. *I wonder if these monks ever bathe?* She brought him a basin of warm water, and began to lay out a generous lunch. Maria lingered over the meal, coaxing the monk to eat just a little more. He happily complied.

Domenicantonio couldn't bear to watch his mother's nervous distress as she hovered around the hungry monk. He turned to loading the cart with his few possessions – some books, a change of clothes, a warm coat. Then, following his father's instructions, he stocked the cart with several casks of good wine, clay urns of olive oil, wheels of cheese, and generous lengths of cured meat, all for the comfort of the monks. No one could say Giustino was not a generous host.

The Family of the Priest

"I am sorry my husband is not here, but the harvest keeps him in the fields." In fact, Giustino had stomped out the door after breakfast without a word.

When it seemed it might almost be too late in the day for them to leave, Fra Marco jumped up, clapped his hands, offered a quick blessing to Maria, and turned to the boy. "We must go. We'll stop in Pietracupa tonight and stay with my sister."

The boy looked at his mother and shrugged slightly.

"Well, I guess it's time," Maria said, smiling tightly.

Domenicantonio hugged his mamma hard. Then she handed him a sack carefully packed with olives, cheese, and bread, and he climbed into the cart. It was a full-day's journey to Trivento, maybe longer by the look of the monk's old mule.

As they pulled away, Maria waved, her heart bursting with sorrow. Half way up the track to the main road, the young boy looked back. He could see his mother biting the back of her hand to control the tears. Then, from the corner of his eye, a shadow darted behind the tree next to the farmhouse. Much later, he learned it had been his father, too proud to show his tears.

Three months passed. For the mamma, it seemed an eternity. For the papà, the sadness was unbearable. Even

The Family of the Priest

the villagers noticed. At least Maria had the church to turn to. Giustino had no one with whom to share his despair. What more could he do? He could not fight the Church. His pride was all he had to hold onto.

Once a month, Maria would leave the farmhouse overnight to visit her mother in Castropignano. On her return, the couple said little to each other. When words were exchanged it was, "Pass the wine…we need more bread…don't bother making me dinner," and so on. Many times, Giustino missed meals altogether or left for work even earlier so he didn't have to comfort his wife. Then one morning, a messenger arrived on horseback with a letter.

"Our son is coming home!"

Giustino lifted his head from his breakfast plate. Tears ran down his face.

"I'm so sorry, cara mia," he sobbed to Maria. "It's my fault! I blamed you all along for wanting our Domenicantonio to become a priest. I blame myself for not being strong enough to insist he stay here. I didn't know what to do. I prayed quietly to God every night to tell me what to do, but he never answered me."

"Here's your answer," she cried, wrapping her arms around her husband's strong neck.

The Family of the Priest

"I know how hard you work," she said. "Well, I've been working hard too. All those days I was away from you, I was taking our good food to our son and your wine to the monks."

"What! You weren't visiting your mother?" Giustino was shocked that his saint had deceived him.

"Yes, yes, I did stop in for a short visit, but I doubled back and went north to see our son." Then she teased. "You know, Husband, the trip was long enough I would have preferred to take our horse instead of riding our donkey. He's as stubborn as you are." Still embracing, the pair laughed together for the first time in months.

The following midday, a tired Domenicantonio arrived home from the long trip and was welcomed by the embraces of his parents. The news travelled fast through the village – the "young priest" was back. The boy wore the attention modestly but comfortably, like a vestment cut to fit. To his parents, Domenicantonio seemed surer of himself. He deliberately served at mass with their old friend, the parish priest, and jumped in to help his father wherever needed. Maria was happy. Giustino could not complain. The two weeks flew by and the boy was off again to study for another six months.

Domenicantonio wasn't the only one changing.

— *The Family of the Priest* —

Giustino began to notice people treating him differently. As he chatted in the fields with his contadini or walked through the village, the greetings were more lofty, the bows more deferential. He noticed he was no longer referred to as one of la famiglia del Feliciani. He now was of la famiglia del prete. His son had created a new branch of the Meffe clan.

At first, this embarrassed him. Then it angered him – why did he merit such respect? What had he achieved? Having a potential priest in the family did not contribute to the family's wealth.

Giustino had never been a religious man – too busy working la terra to attend mass except at Christmas and Easter, but now he felt a deep sense of guilt that he had ignored his devotion to the Church.

While he struggled with his new role, Maria blossomed into hers. She became even more devout, tending the sick, taking meals to the elderly, and depositing every coin she saved into the alms box at the back of the church.

Giustino, meanwhile, began to sink into his old ways. He couldn't stop the growing hurt he felt that his son had chosen God over family and farm. It made no sense. You couldn't see God. You couldn't feel him like the fine soil he filtered through his fingers. *How do we know God is there?* Despair overwhelmed him.

Oh, my God. What am I thinking? Forgive me. Have mercy on me. Please send me a sign of what I should do.

Most days, Giustino set aside his inner misgivings in order to carry on. He couldn't display his doubts in the village – it would cause trouble – so he let on that he was pleased with his newfound prestige. *There must be another way to persuade my boy that working the land is God's work too.*

On one of his son's visits, he walked Domenicantonio through the workshop where new wine casks, taller than a man, were being made. "We're up to 30 barrels of wine a year," he said to his son. "Someday, all this will be yours. Think of what we can achieve together." A few minutes later, he added, "What kind of life is the Church going to give you?"

The two men continued walking in silence. Then Domenicantonio turned and gently placing his hand on his father's shoulder said, "Papà, you don't understand how infinite God is. A few barrels of wine or parcels of land are like grains of sand to Him. God gives His love to all the people in the world. We feed a few dozen people here."

The Family of the Priest

A gentle shift was happening between the two men. The authority of the father was slipping as the son gained spiritual and intellectual confidence. Sometimes a contadino could be heard greeting "Don Domenico" in acknowledgement of the son's growing respect in the community.

Giustino chose not to notice. Instead, his arguments became more creative and more persistent with each of his son's visits home. Perhaps Domenicantonio could find a tutor close to the village so he could study and work at the same time. Perhaps he could assist the local priest and live at home.

Sometimes, Giustino was more direct. "What about all the people who depend on us? Who will run the estate when I'm gone?"

"Papà, there are more than enough people to work."

Over the years, resignation gradually pushed down disappointment. For the priest's father, it seemed once again that a vineyard was no match for God's Church.

Perhaps it was at one of the shelters that mark the crossroads on the way to Trivento, or it could have been in the coach on his way back to school, that 20-year-old Domenicantonio encountered the most beautiful, young woman he had ever seen. In the presence of a

The Family of the Priest

chaperone, we can imagine how intently they spoke that first day. They spoke of God's work, of history and art, and, of the great philosophers. Her modesty, intelligence, and devotion were as attractive to the young man as her fine figure. They exchanged names and family backgrounds. He learned she was the daughter of an influential merchant from Boiano in the south, on her way to visit an aunt in Trivento. He was surprised she was so far from home. She was surprised he was attending the monastery! When they parted, he felt as if every nerve in his body was alive – colours were brighter, smells more intense – the smallest sound amplified. He had much to contemplate when later he knelt with the monks in silent prayer.

In the closed world of the Italian countryside, there are no secrets. The coachman would have noticed the young people talking and would tell his wife. She would tell her sister, who would tell the priest's housekeeper, who would whisper it to Maria's cousin, who passed it on to Maria at the end of mass, who would bring it home to her husband. This was the miracle Giustino had prayed for!

"So, figlio, who is this girl we hear about?" At first Domenicantonio denied there was anything to talk about, but he couldn't hide his growing attachment to the beautiful girl. We'll call her Angelina, for her name has been lost to the story. The pair wrote long letters, back and forth. Giustino encouraged the relationship at every opportunity, laughing to himself as he remembered the chance meeting of another young couple, so long ago. Maria, too, saw what was happening and said little. She quietly reminded him of his upcoming vow of celibacy. She prayed even harder for her son to resist temptation, but for the first time, Maria doubted the strength of her will. Something stronger possessed her son – impossible for even a good mother to fight. All these years of love, prayer, and effort would be wasted. Was this her pride speaking? Could she be wrong about her son? Did God have other plans for her boy?

Domenicantonio continued his studies, but the more he thought about Angelina, the more he doubted his vocation. Was he truly called to be a priest? He was a healthy, young man attracted to a beautiful, young woman. Never had he known such deep longing! His concentration lapsed. Studying became impossible. It wasn't long before the change in his behaviour came to the attention of his superiors at the monastery. Naturally, they were worried and tried to speak with him, but he resisted their attempts, determined to settle this dilemma himself.

The Family of the Priest

One morning after Matins, it came to him like a strong wind straight from the Holy Spirit. Domenicantonio would do his father's bidding. He would marry, start a family, and share the responsibility of the estate with his father, just as his father had done before him. He planned to tell his parents on his next visit home.

The months seemed to never pass. Most nights he lay awake, in pain, dreaming of his sweet Angelina. The days were relieved only by the occasional letter from his intended bride.

Then, at once, the letters stopped. First, a week went by, then another, and another, with no word from his beloved. As he packed his things, preparing to go home and change the course of his life, his thoughts raced ahead excitedly. *Why had he not heard from Angelina in so many weeks?*

It took only minutes to discover the answer. Upon entering the farmhouse, mamma handed him a letter. *Why was it delivered to the farmhouse and not to the monastery? Perhaps she had anticipated his arrival home.* He opened the letter and began to read.

My dearest Dom,
This is the happiest yet saddest day of my life. I have met a wonderful, young man from Boiano…

The Family of the Priest

The cup of wine slipped from his hand shattering on the stone floor. Disbelief compelled him to read on.

I love you very much as a friend, but now realize that you aspire to a much higher calling. While I still have intense feelings for you, my feelings for my new love are even stronger. Like you, he is a good man and together we plan to raise a family and be very happy. I would be honoured to have you bless our marriage....

"Enough!" he roared, crumpling the letter and holding it over the candle. As his parents watched, he tossed the burning paper into the fire and laughed bitterly, "Ashes to ashes, dust to dust." He rose, blew out the candle, and strode out of the farmhouse. The next day, he returned to the monastery.

Why had the girl rejected him? Had her parents steered her away from the young seminarian out of fear for their immortal souls? Surely they were risking God's wrath if they allowed their daughter to marry a man chosen for God. It was common belief that if you robbed God, He will rob you ten times over. Your crops will fail. Your children will be crippled. Your animals will die.

Domenicantonio buried himself in his studies to purge his anger and bitterness. When he returned home, he wore the black cassock of a priest, although he was not yet ordained. His visits were purposefully short, for fear he would argue with his father.

Finally, in 1815, Domenicantonio was blessed by the bishop and raised up as a deacon, the last major step before being anointed as a priest of the Roman Catholic Church. Maria whispered a heartfelt thank you to the Blessed Virgin. It seemed "The Family of the Priest" was now a reality.

Like a returning war hero, Domenicantonio entered Torella del Sannio to countless bows and kisses, cheers and handshakes. That evening, more than 100 villagers gathered at the family farmhouse for a celebration unlike any other. The wine flowed, the bagpipes played, no plate stayed empty, no person stood still. The young deacon smiled, and kept his sadness to himself.

CHAPTER FIVE

Tragedy

With a glance up at the crucified image, Domenicantonio walked out of the sanctuary. Puzzled whispers rippled through the church.

Domenicantonio came home regularly during those final months before his ordination to help out his old friend, the parish priest. He assisted at Holy Communion, blessed the sick, and preached the homily. On one visit, "the young priest" was met at the door by his mother, out of her mind with worry.

"Your father left three days ago to check the far reaches of our land, but he only had food for a day and a night. Something is wrong! I know it," she wailed.

If there was much work to be done, it was normal for him to stay away one night, or even two, at one of the farm's *rifugi*. He could make a fire, boil some potatoes, and sleep comfortably. But staying out longer than two nights was unusual because he knew how much Maria hated to be alone.

The Family of the Priest

"Maybe he's fallen and injured himself," the son offered.

"Or he has been murdered by *brigandi!*" These were lawless times in Italy, when gangs of bandits took advantage of the political uncertainty after the French lost control of the Kingdom of the Two Sicilies.

"More likely the horse has gone lame."

"Or someone has cursed us with the *malocchio!*" She wailed even harder, clutching the long, pepper-shaped charm hanging around her neck.

"Now, now, mamma, I am sure there's a good reason why he is late. I'll call some of the men. We'll find him."

Several hours passed. Maria prayed. She paced. She prayed some more and then, she started to cook. *The men will be hungry.* The action of preparing a meal calmed her.

Then, just after dark, Domenicantonio slowly entered the farmhouse and dropped into a chair.

"Figlio mio, what is it? Where is your father? Is he hurt?"

Without looking at his mother, he said dully, "He's gone. It's over. I just gave papà last rites."

They collapsed into each other arms in a rush of tears and raw emotion. A farm worker had found Giustino beside a stream. There were no marks on his body. No sign of injury or foul play. He'd probably stopped for a drink and his heart gave out. Such a tragedy and only 56 years old.

The young deacon assisted at his own father's funeral, fighting back his emotions as he spoke the eulogy. He told the villagers how Giustino Meffe was a great man, a man of honour, the epitome of hard work, a man devoted to his family, and an equally caring padrone. It was the hardest thing he had ever had to do. He kept telling himself, *I am almost a priest now. I must show courage and leadership*, and that included not crying at his father's funeral.

Most people realize their mistakes in life when it is too late and Domenicantonio was no exception. In the months that followed, he seldom slept well. He blamed himself for his father's premature death – certain Giustino had died of a broken heart, exhausted and abandoned. *If only I had helped him more with the farm. If only I had been more patient and understanding of my father's ways.*

He was wracked with guilt. He prayed constantly,

"Dear God, what if I had helped him instead of leaving him alone? Would you have taken him so soon?"

By necessity, his mother took over running the estate. But it quickly became clear that her inexperience put his father's life's work at risk.

He returned to the seminary filled with conflicting emotions. Guilt turned to bitterness, and then to anger. He raged against God. *Why am I being punished for following my Saviour?* His fellow priests chastised him, counselling him about God's mysterious ways. "You must accept your fate and maintain your faith." In the end, Domenicantonio could not.

Just weeks away from his final vows, as he co-celebrated the mass of the six-month anniversary of his father's death, Domenicantonio looked out at the parishioners. He held up his hand and murmured the Latin blessing.

"*Benedícat vos omnípotens Deus, Pater, Fílius et Spíritus Sanctus.*"

"*Amen,*" responded the faithful.

With his back to the congregation, he slowly pulled the lace-trimmed surplice over his head, folded it, kissed it, and placed it on the altar beside the large missal. *Father, my life has been Yours from the moment of my birth. I have given You so much and my earthly father, so little. But now, I know what I must do. Please forgive me for what I have done and what I am about to do.* Then he pulled the starched, white collar from around his neck, placed it on the altar, and with a glance up at the crucified image, Domenicantonio walked out of the sanctuary by the side door. Puzzled whispers rippled through the church.

Domenicantonio would never again return to the altar, never celebrate the Eucharist as a priest. For the first time in his life, he made a decision for the benefit of no one but himself.

CHAPTER SIX
A New Life

In 1821, a first son was born and named Giustino after the bridegroom's father. Five more children followed. Everyone seemed happy as the family of the priest grew.

Like the seasons, Domenicantonio's life had come full circle. There was no more conflict. His purpose was clear – honour his late father's memory, take over the estate, and look after his mother. Life was simple. Work. Eat. Sleep.

The parish priest visited the mother and son often. Their talks were warm and friendly, with the priest coaxing Domenicantonio to keep his heart open to God.

"You have no idea what the Father has planned for you."

"Oh, I think I know what the Father plans – long days working in the hot sun and the many headaches that go with running this place!"

"Maybe so, but if you could spare a few hours for your old friend, I could use your help."

"How can I help you, Don? I have turned my back on God."

"You have changed your mind. There is no sin in that. You are still more a man of God than most in these parts and there is much to be done among His people." And so the almost-priest joined the parish priest in assisting with the minor duties of the parish.

Domenicantonio was now in his thirties, his mother, in her sixties, and so Maria's prayers took a new tack.

"Figlio mio, who knows how much longer I will be with you."

"Mamma! Please. You will outlive me."

"No, let me finish. Figlio, you are a man, still strong and young enough. You need a wife to look after your needs and to give me grandchildren before I die!"

Gradually his mother's persistence penetrated his gloomy thinking. *Maybe my mother is right. I should find a wife.* He remembered seeing a lovely young woman at mass in his mother's village of Castropignano. There was something compelling about her. Desire surprised him and so did old thoughts of Angelina. Perhaps it *was* time to move forward. He was the padrone, not the prete and there was nothing to stop him from seeking the young woman's attentions.

Very little is known of Teresa Borsella, the woman who would eventually become the wife of the priest. For the sake of this story I have imagined her history – made her a beauty, a beauty with a burden. Like so many young women of the day, Teresa had been promised to the son of a neighbouring family and the two children had grown up knowing they would someday be spouses. Then at 16, the boy suddenly left Castropignano. One of his mother's elderly uncles, an old bachelor in Naples, needed an apprentice. The boy's mother insisted he take this opportunity to break his bondage to the land and so the marriage contract was cancelled. The boy's family paid heavily for his freedom and Teresa was left behind.

At first, she was devastated by the shame of rejection, but then, she started to think, *Why shouldn't I have more from life than this miseria?* She was a clever girl and had learned to read and write. Whenever she finished her chores, she could be found with a book in hand.

While some might have regarded her as unmarriageable, her beauty continued to attract the attention of a series of young men from the village in the years following the broken engagement. She refused them all, much to her father's growing frustration. He had four more daughters to marry off and until Teresa was gone, their lives were on hold. And as she entered her twenties, he began to despair that he would die in a household of spinsters.

To say Domenicantonio's appearance at the Borsella home was a godsend is understating its impact on Teresa's family! Within days of their meeting, Domenicantonio and his future father-in-law had settled on the terms of her dowry. Teresa seemed content with the situation. Here was a man who could give her a chance at a better life.

And so, in 1819, at the age of 35, Domenicantonio Meffe married 22-year-old Teresa Borsella.

On the morning of the ceremony, the bridal couple met in front of the parish priest to take Holy Communion and receive his blessing. The bride wore a white blouse delicately trimmed in hand-knotted lace. The bodice of her dress, apron, and head scarf were black and red, decorated with brilliantly-coloured embroidery. The elaborate gold earrings adorning her ears were a gift from her mother-in-law and meant to ward off the evil eye. The groom may have carried a piece of iron in his trousers as his talisman. As they left the church, symbols of good fortune surrounded them – two small, potted olive trees, their initials scrawled on the church steps, and in the local tradition, villagers broke bread over their heads to bring them many children.

They say it was the biggest, most wonderful wedding anyone had seen in years. Two hundred guests sang and danced the intricate steps of the tarantella. They ate and raised their glasses repeatedly, encouraging the couple to make Maria a nonna!

Maria welcomed the young woman into her home, and though she sometimes found her daughter-in-law headstrong and too vocal with her opinions, they got along well, especially when Teresa began producing grandchildren.

In 1821, a first son was born and named Giustino Meffe after the bridegroom's father. In 1823, a second son, Donato, was born, and in 1825, a third son, Francesco, arrived. Three more children followed. Everyone seemed happy as the family of the priest grew. Domenicantonio was delighted to be the patriarch of such a fine brood. Teresa proved to be a hardworking, devoted wife and mother. And Maria loved the activity in her once-silent home. She had every reason to be content this late in life. God seemed to be smiling on the Meffe family of the priest.

For the next 13 years, life was beautiful. For the first time in his life, Domenicantonio felt content. No longer did he feel the tension of wondering where he belonged and what he was supposed to be doing. His path was clear. He had the love of a good woman and sons that would follow him. The harvests were good. The estate was doing well. He acquired more land, grew more wheat, planted more vines and olive trees, expanded his flocks, and turned all his energy towards building on his father's work, and the work of his father before him.

As with everything on the estate, the tending of the vineyards varied with the season. In the cold months of January and February, the vines were dormant. This was the time to cut wood, so it would be dry by summer to make more wine barrels. Typically, the barrels lasted about 50 years and Domenicantonio's dated from his father's day, so the time had come for him to replace the old ones and make new ones. With such a large family, he wanted to increase production and make sure each child would have two barrels of fine wine as part of their inheritance.

～ *The Family of the Priest* ～

Domenicantonio was proud of his children, especially his three older boys, who already showed the kind of willingness to learn the customs of the land that he had withheld from his own father.

"Papà would be so happy," he said wistfully to his wife. Donato, the second son, was hardworking and clever with numbers, and Francesco, the third, was always ready with a song or a helping hand, however, it was his firstborn, Giustino, who made his heart swell with pride. Giustino had inherited the best qualities of his grandparents, their strength and spirituality, and none of his parents' hotheadedness.

And so it was that on a cool, gusty, February morning, young Giustino headed out with his father to the valley. He was feeling well-pleased that his papà had picked him alone to come along. The other boys clamoured their protests, but Domenicantonio was emphatic, "I don't need distractions cutting trees. I need real help," patting his eldest's dark head. Twenty-five men set out on horse-drawn wagons to cut down several of the great oaks.

Near the end of the day, a powerful gust of wind caught a tree not completely cut and propelled it in the wrong direction. As it rolled and bounced, men yelled and ran from its path. The young Giustino, who at that moment was bent down drinking from a stream, must not have heard it. The tree crushed him before he knew what had happened.

Domenicantonio watched in horror, his feet rooted to the ground. It was the anguish of his own voice that propelled him forward, like the howling of the last wolf in Molise. The men worked frantically to cut away the branches imprisoning the boy, all the while Domenicantonio whispered, "Hold on Giustino. I am here. We'll get you out. Hold on. Hold on." At last, he gently brushed away the leaves to reveal the sweet, young face. The boy was so pale, so still.

Once freed from his leafy bed, he scooped the boy in his arms and carried him the four kilometres to the village, petitioning every saint he could think of for mercy. As he climbed the steps to the church, he felt certain God would save his son. He pushed open the door and staggered down the centre aisle towards the nave, his footsteps echoing in the semidarkness. As he entered the sanctuary, he paused, bowed before the crucified Christ, and offered his suffering to the Lord. Gently, he laid Giustino on the great marble altar beneath the reclining figure of Torella's patron, San Clemente, the pope and martyr. And in that moment, he saw what he had refused to believe.

Domenicantonio could not explain to Teresa and his mother how the tree fell or how long it took the men to release their boy from its hold. He could say nothing about his entreaties to San Clemente or the rest of the heavenly brethren. His only offering was the broken body tenderly placed on the kitchen table.

There was no reaching him in his grief. Teresa wept with him. Maria murmured comfort. The priest came. Even the new baby could not raise Domenicantonio from the depths of his despair. His precious first born, named for the father he had caused so much pain, was dead at age 13.

Then as if losing a son were not enough, his beloved mother faded away. Maria never recovered from young Giustino's death. In the sad days after the funeral, she grew more tired and less able to get around, until one morning Teresa went to her room to find her mother-in-law dead in her bed. No one doubted that she died of a broken heart.

Domenicantonio retreated into himself. For two years, he spoke to no one, went nowhere – not to town, not to church, not to the fields. God had taken his son to punish him for his selfishness, for putting his family before the priesthood. Teresa tried reaching out to him,

The Family of the Priest

but he rejected her warmth. She grieved her son in her own way by keeping busy and looking after the rest of the brood. In quiet moments late at night, she began to blame her husband for their boy's death.

The months turned to years with agonizing slowness, and gradually, Domenicantonio went back to work, often leaving before sunrise and coming home after dark, eating alone and rarely speaking. His family hovered quietly in the background, staying out of his way, making no demands. People avoided the dark and joyless house of la famiglia del prete. Even Teresa found reasons to be away. Although she could easily have afforded a woman to wash her sheets, she enjoyed making the daily trip to the well, sharing in the vitality of the other women and the gossip of continuing life in the village. She sometimes went out on the land herself, speaking to the foremen, trying to understand how the great estate operated.

Domenicantonio, steeped in self-absorption, saw none of this until Donato, his second son, tentatively approached him. Donato had filled his father's shoes on the estate out of necessity and not preparedness. And yet as he drew closer to his father, there was fear in his eyes. In his darkest moments, Domenicantonio had angrily lashed out at his boys more than once over the years, even raising his fists against Teresa and her sharp tongue. When Domenicantonio realized the young man before him was expecting a fight, he saw for the first time how strong Donato had become. *He's no boy. He's a man. And I am not sure I could stand up to him.*

"Father, I am 22. I have been working since I was a little boy. There is a young woman from the village I want to marry and I need your blessing."

"Go on. Tell me about her." The boy made him smile when he talked of how he felt at the sight of his bride-to-be. *What a burden I have become. This is no way to treat the family I once professed to love so much. They need me.*

In 1845, the two young people were married. The wedding reminded many of the celebration decades before when their padrone had almost become a priest.

In 1846, Donato's first son was born and named Giustino for his brother killed by the falling tree. And now the story begins to come closer to my own era. This Giustino was my great-grandfather, the namesake of my own father. This Giustino talked with my ancestor before the old "priest" died. Then, when Giustino grew old, he told his son, my grandfather, the story before my great-grandfather died in 1914.

CHAPTER SEVEN

From Joy to Rage

Teresa grew tired of her husband's endless self-blame, his dark rantings against God, and his long lapses into silence. Any attempt to reach him was rejected. After years of trying, she simply gave up and went on with her life.

There was nothing Domenicantonio loved more than being with the grandson that bore the name of his lost son and the father he missed so much. The child's innocence penetrated his murky world.

As he entered his seventh decade, the patriarch began to find life's daily chores more and more difficult. His hands became twisted with arthritis, and sometimes his back and knees were so sore that he had to rest to recover. He drank more wine to ease the pain. Yet when he chased little Giustino around the farmhouse or hid with him among the wine barrels, the aches and pains vanished.

Then Donato would laugh and tell his wife, "Look at papà. He's like a little child."

"Stop him Donato. He'll hurt himself."

"Take it easy papà. We don't want you to have a fit."

In these moments Donato saw the father he remembered prior to his brother's death, a father he had loved deeply.

Hand in hand, the grandfather and the little boy took long walks across the fields and through the village. Domenicantonio told him endless stories of the joy and tragedy of his youthful years. They counted as they climbed the 73 steps to the church of San Nicola di Bari, sometimes going inside to talk to God.

"What should I say to him, Tatone?" little Giustino whispered to his grandfather.

"Shh, quiet. People are trying to pray. God will get angry if you make too much noise in his house." The little boy frowned and buried his head in his hands.

With his grandson at his side, the old man prayed. "Dear Lord, please forgive me for my many sins, especially the anger and hatred that have poisoned my life. Please let my grandson live. He has done nothing to hurt You or anyone. Please give him health and protect the rest of my children and grandchildren. I now know why You took my first son and I beg that with Your mercy I will soon join him in Your presence.

I am old. Please take me Lord and let my family live on in Your glory."

The estate continued to prosper and as Domenicantonio and Teresa's children moved to neighbouring villages to begin families of their own, they in turn carried the name, la famiglia del prete. Truly, it seemed like the priest's prayers were answered.

Donato was now busy running the great estate, living in his own home on land that his father deeded him. He'd stop in occasionally to pay his respects to his parents. On the big feast days and at harvest, they'd see the rest of the family, but more often than not, the old priest and his wife found themselves alone. Teresa's work around the house never stopped, but the old man had little to do and it wore on him.

"Why don't they come any more?" Domenicantonio complained.

"They're busy. It's far. Stop moaning," Teresa would shout back.

"Too busy to visit the parents who gave them life?"

"You wanted grandchildren. You got them. Count your blessings."

The Family of the Priest

In the early years of their marriage, the 13-year difference in their ages seemed meaningless; now Teresa's 59 seemed so young to his 72. In many ways, she was still an energetic and attractive woman. When the family did get together, she was the centre of attention, while the old priest sat in the corner reworking the pain of the past, hardly speaking. Sometimes he cried for no apparent reason or he'd forget what he intended to say. Other times, he'd be talkative and content and then suddenly anxious and reclusive. He began to resent Teresa's energy and went back to his old ways, avoiding her by staying out all day. If she asked him what he was doing, he'd simply say, "I was working." She knew it was a lie.

Once the couple had known great passion and joy as they raised their family and worked the estate. Tragedy could have brought them closer, but instead, it pushed them apart. Teresa grew tired of her husband's endless self-blame, his dark rantings against God, and his long lapses into silence. Any attempt to reach him was rejected. Any special attention went unacknowledged. After years of trying, she simply gave up and went on with her life. She wondered, *Was this how their last years together were to unfold, distant and empty?*

One day, Domenicantonio came across his wife talking with one of the foremen from the estate while out in the fields. He hurried out of view and found a spot to relieve himself. Walking back from the bushes he noticed how closely they stood and the intensity of their conversation. He said nothing to his wife when she returned home. He resolved to watch her with more care.

In those days, it was a crime for a woman to dishonour her family by having an affair. In fact, in the eyes of the law it was understandable and excusable for a husband to kill an adulterous wife. The community's honour was as much at stake as the husband's.

The more he thought about Teresa's behaviour, the more his blood boiled. How could she betray him? She was the wife of an ex-priest! What he had seen was enough for some men, but he needed proof of Teresa's infidelity. His opportunity came a few days later. Teresa announced she was going to the land to gather vegetables for supper. He grunted in acknowledgement. Moments after she left, he followed her at a safe distance. His faculties were not so sharp these days and his vision was poor, but he knew this was not the way to the land!

Suspicion began to cloud his already confused mind. He watched her every move, analyzing every word she spoke for hidden meaning. As weeks passed, his suspicions grew. Another trip to the land. Again, he followed her and again she took the same route. *What the hell was going on?* On the next trip, he edged closer, hiding behind a clump of trees. It was Teresa, unmistakably embracing the foreman.

Rage raced through his body followed quickly by disbelief, then certainty. *No honourable woman touched another man. What about her religion? She couldn't possibly be having an affair. It would bring shame and ridicule on the entire family.* But he also knew how hot-blooded his wife was, though their bed had long grown cold. He doubted she could resist the temptation of a younger, more attentive man.

He watched, horrified, as his wife drank from the flagon of wine and then held it to the other man's lips. In that moment, his breath exploded as though he'd been punched in the stomach. This intimate act was a prelude to something unspeakable!

His heart pounded with pure hatred. He envisioned himself plunging a pitchfork into the man's chest as Teresa watched.

The fifth commandment, *Thou shalt not kill,* and the sixth commandment, *Thou shalt not commit adultery* paralyzed him. He fell weakly to his knees. Unable to walk, he crawled to the bushes and wept. *Again God, You take away my life?*

For days, he gravitated between rage and confusion. *Why are You punishing me once again? You give me a grandson and take away my wife? Is it because I left Your church? I left Your family, so You're taking away mine? Is that how it works?*

But his rage was short-lived. Too old and too tired, he simply didn't care anymore. "Do what You will," he repeated. "I'm just an old man. Maybe I did abandon my father and the church. Fine! Then punish me accordingly. Just don't punish my children or grandchildren."

At least now he knew the truth. And the truth was this affair would be a smear on his entire family, on the reputation of la famiglia del prete. Could he blame his wife? Had he been much of a husband these so many years?

He considered confronting her. Mostly though, half-formed thoughts careened in his head and made it impossible to follow a clear path. Then Teresa herself provided the resolution – another outing and another opportunity to verify that his eyes had not tricked him. He followed her and once more, he saw them embrace.

The Family of the Priest

This was not a bad dream. This was the cruel truth and it required a cruel answer – to kill them both.

Indecision immobilized him. He was a former man of God, not a murderer. What could he do? Hope they were discreet? Do nothing and risk the family's honour if the affair became public? Confronting Teresa would only make things worse. The lovers would still see each other. There must be a way to end this diplomatically. He would do everything possible to end the affair and preserve the respect for la famiglia del prete.

On a windy November afternoon, the ex-priest and his wife were startled by a deafening clap of thunder, followed by wild flashes of lightning and torrents of rain. No one would visit on a night like this. Teresa went to the fireplace, put on a few extra logs, and began to cook. The water boiled briskly in the big copper pot, ready for the potatoes. Everything seemed so calm, so routine.

Domenicantonio busied himself taking apart some old chairs. "What are you doing?" yelled Teresa.

"Look. These chairs are falling apart. They need to be fixed." He placed one end of the palete, a long metal rod, into the fire. Once hot, he used it to burn holes in the legs of the chair, so they could be reinforced with horizontal braces, a job he'd done many times before. To properly burn the holes in the chair, the metal of the palete must be red hot.

He blew into the scisciaturo to fan the flames in the fireplace. Holding the first chair between his knees, he poked the hot metal into the chair leg. Smoke filled the room. He felt dizzy. Sweat poured from his face.

Teresa bent over the fire, pricking the potatoes to see if they were done. Glancing over her shoulder she asked, "What are you doing?"

In that same moment he was behind her. He lifted her skirt and thrust the burning iron deep inside her. Just as quickly, he pulled it out. She screamed and then fell, gasping for air, shaking uncontrollably. Her lips turned blue.

The old man closed his eyes in disbelief. When he opened them again, she was still there. The stench of scorched flesh was hers.

He knelt beside her. She grabbed his hand tightly. She couldn't stop shaking. Her eyes told him she didn't know what had happened.

"Don. Father," she gasped. "Please. Bless me before I go to our son."

His tears mingled with hers as he recited the prayers for the dying. "I am so sorry Teresa."

With a last gasp and a shudder, she slipped away. Tenderly, he took ashes from the hearth, and with his thumb traced the sign of the cross on her forehead. By the grace of God, her sins were forgiven.

CHAPTER EIGHT
And Now

*On good days, he walked into the village,
went to mass or sat in the piazza with the other old men.
His frequent conversations with God grew simpler
as he begged for forgiveness.*

HE stayed with his wife for a long time before he headed into the storm to look for help. Neighbours came immediately. People were certain it had been her heart. There wasn't a mark on her body. When they buried her, Teresa was the honoured wife of the respected ex-priest.

The old man continued to live in the house, steeped in his memories. A local woman, paid to come daily to bring him his food, swept the hearth and washed his soiled linens. Occasionally, one of his children or grandchildren stopped by to visit. On good days, he walked to the village, went to mass or sat in the piazza with the other old men.

One day, either in confusion or guilt, he let it slip to his grandson, Giustino, that *he* was responsible for the death of Nonna Teresa. "That's crazy, nonno!" He knew his grandfather often became confused, but this seemed too far-fetched.

Yet each visit revealed more and more details of the old man's actions and left Giustino stunned. Often, Domenicantonio wept uncontrollably, his tears making his story more believable, so much so that Giustino began to think maybe it *was* true. Unsettled, he kept his thoughts to himself. Eventually, the old priest told the young man the entire story.

In the last few months of his life, Domenicantonio's frequent conversations with God grew simpler as he begged for forgiveness. When he finally died, he seemed at peace.

But the story doesn't end there. When Giustino and his wife began to have children, they named their first son Donato, after Giustino's own father. Their second son, born in 1885, bore the name of his great-grandfather, the priest, Domenicantonio. That Domenicantonio was my beloved grandfather. Before my grandfather died in 1962, he told me what his father had learned from the priest at the end of his life. In my grandfather's version, the story always stopped before its horrific climax. It was my father, fixing a chair, who revealed the ending. He had come to see us in Italy after five years in Canada and wanted to stay, but when he saw how little had changed in Torella, he knew he had to bring us all to Toronto.

At the time, the story seemed both terrible and wonderful, but I was just an immigrant boy poised on the edge of unimaginable excitement and thought little of it. I was more interested in exploring the opportunities that my new life presented. Now that so many years have passed, experience feeds my commitment to prevent the history of my ancestors from being lost in the wind. I feel it is my obligation, my contribution to my heritage, to bring to life the story of the priest's family, not only for the sake of my family and for the Torellesi, but for the whole world to know.

The Meffe family has continued to grow, as siblings in subsequent generations had large families of their own. Today the Family of the Priest numbers in the many hundreds. Few remain in Molise. Most immigrated to Canada, the US, Argentina, England and Belgium, and with distance and time, the priest's story has faded. This has motivated me to sift for the truth through the memories of the oldest members of the family before they passed. What I present is what I have been able to determine and it is this that I pass on to my own children. They may be too young to be very interested, and this may or may not change when they reach my age. In any event, I have kept the promise of my heart and know that I can live out the rest of my life certain that this great family story lives on.

Why, 200 years later, bother sharing it? Some in the family will be shocked by its brutality and would rather see it forgotten. Undoubtedly, they will be upset with me for bringing it to light, however, this is not merely a story of murder. This is a story of great passion, a story of spiritual struggle and a story of accomplishment in an era when most rural Italians thought little beyond the necessities of life. It should be embraced, not buried and, in doing so, by accepting the glory of the past we are compelled to accept its grit – otherwise we cheat and deal in only half-truths.

I am not proud of the worst of my ancestor's deeds, but I am proud of his best. None of us are blameless. His sins are not mine. We take the good with the bad and in the end, understand fully what it means to be of la famiglia del prete.

Church of San Nicola di Bari, Torella.

Acknowledgements

MANY people along the way have helped me with this project. As well as the family members already mentioned, thank you to writer Deborah Verginella and poet Pier Giorgio Di Cicco, former Poet Laureate of Toronto, for their helpful comments on later drafts. Marc Lerman, Director of Archives for the Archdiocese of Toronto, provided advice on 19th century clerical vestments.

My writer, Bernadette Hardaker, found Mary Melfi's 2009 book, <u>Italy Revisited: Conversations with My Mother</u> very useful, as was the website by the same name. Many of the food references and local traditions came from that site. It also has an excellent selection of photographs and artwork that evoke the period of the

Acknowledgements

book. <u>Peasant Art in Italy,</u> edited by Charles Holme and published in 1913 had useful costume references. Carlo Levi's 1949 book, <u>Christ Stopped at Eboli</u> was very helpful and is the source for the story of the Grassano postman. See *torelladelsannio.blog.tiscali.it* for a view of Torella today.

And finally, but most importantly, I must thank my wonderful wife, Carmela, who also grew up in Torella, and as a woman, knows better than most what it must have been like to wander outside the social conventions of the day. For 10 years after my father's death I had a file open containing bits and pieces of my history. In November 2002, while doing the 25-hour drive to Florida, I told Carmela the entire story for the first time. She took notes and it is from those notes that this project began. Without her constant support and encouragement it never would have been finished.

www.ingramcontent.com/pod-product-compliance
Lightning Source LLC
Chambersburg PA
CBHW031425290426
44110CB00011B/533